Deeper Than the Eyes Can See

Barbara J. Love

ISBN: 978-1-7354394-4-0

DEDICATION

To a Great Woman of Courage
When we met, it was an interpersonal relationship. We've had our ups and downs, but you have still stood on solid ground with me. You named my book to fit: "Who Am I! Deeper Than the Eyes Can See." For this, I'm so grateful to know you. Mrs. Erica Banks Motely, you are a sweetheart and a true woman of God.

CONTENTS

ACKNOWLEDGMENTS

To my Dearest Friend

Ms. Misty Salter, you have been with me through the hard times as well as the good times. You have had my back and believed in me when I didn't believe in myself. For that, I thank you.

To my Friend/Sister in Christ

Mrs. Sabrina Coffey—from day one when we met, we were joined by the hip. You made me realize the heart I have for people. You taught me knowledge of who I am. You taught me to have an open mind to everything. You taught me forgiveness to others and to show love. You have always prayed with me and told me I was going to make a difference. You said, "Stand tall. Keep your head up! Never let anyone steal your joy. Follow your dreams." For that, I love you.

♦INTRODUCTION♦

The studies state that many women being mentally, physically, sexually, and verbally abused. Most women are confused, scared, and unsure about wanting to live, so they don't know what to do.

If ever planning to leave, there are steps to take to get out. Therefore, never tell him you're leaving. Do the 3 Ps:

      1.   Plan—take important papers and a small suitcase out to a safe home.

      2.   Prepare—only tell somewhere close to you where you are going.

      3.   Protect—yourself as well as children and keep low for a while.

These P's will assure that your process of choosing life over death will follow you through a way of healing.

When I look back over my life, I see pain, mistakes, and heartaches. When I look in the mirror, I see my life. I see strength, learned lessons, and pride in myself because I'm still here and I'm still moving forward.

Years were passing and I was making the change from living the country life to living the city life. I was so disturbed and angry with myself because I felt all alone. I had very low self-esteem, but mischievous within. I was bullied at school by a girl named Rita on the basketball team. I was 14 years old and dark-skinned and Rita was 14 and high yellow.

She was prejudiced toward dark-skinned girls and I was her pick. My hair was nappy, but I still got a press and curl. I was so tired of being harassed that I bleached my skin, trying to become light-skinned. In the 90s, my attitude toward people was intolerable. I was always angry, fighting, and disrespectful. That was the only way that I felt I could deal with life... If I only trusted myself, then I couldn't get hurt.

Now I was hurt to my soul as a child and as a teenager. People were constantly degrading me, and it was fun for them because they knew it would get to me.

My attitude is different now. I am focused on managing my goals and that will come from having a structure, keeping myself on track, and knowing how to keep priorities in order.

♦YOU DON'T KNOW MY STORY♦

See me being me, I'm a roller coaster ride. I'm Barbara Love—a people person who loves the Lord, a leader over my destiny, and a team player. My hometown is Hernando, Mississippi, and I'm happy to be from down south. I'm a hairstylist that experienced a lot over the last 30 years of my career. My job requires me to analyze people as their Counselor, Stylist, Friend, and create the Style that will better suit them best. My Motto: Hair Care for The Classy Lady!

My birthday is October 14, 1970, which makes me 49 years old. I am a single mother of (2) Tamesha (31), and Gregory (25)— as well as a Godmother to Dominique (38), have three grandkids—Jominque (19), Jermani (11), and Itali (1).

Despite all of God's obstacles, I know I was put here on earth for a reason. My hobbies are singing, dancing, and drama. Also, I enjoy working with the community centers because allows me the opportunity to arrange different activities and events for our youth. I currently teach etiquette classes are once a month, CPR classes once a year. I also take them to jamborees and on out of town trips. Another part of what I do is visiting juvenile facilities at the penal farm in Memphis, TN for attitude adjustments.

I graduated from Southaven High School in Southaven, Mississippi in 1989. In the same year, I graduated from IBA School of Cosmetology. Later, I received a Bachelor of Psychology from the University of Phoenix. My community service accolades are as follows: one of the 50 Women Who Make a Difference in the Community, member of Salons against Domestic Violence, and sponsor of the Dynamic Dymond & Blazin' Dolls Majorettes, Professionally, I have taught at Tennessee Academy of Cosmetology and New Wave Hair Academy, served as director of Miss Irene International Salon and Spa. I am also a foster parent for Youth

Villages and Meritan. Growth made me the person I am today!

My story begins as a 6-year-old girl living in Hernando, Mississippi. I lived in a trailer house with my mother Lynn, stepfather Rodney, sister Reece, and

two brothers, Kalvin and Roderick. We went to Hope P. Sullivan Elementary. We had to be bused from our house Southaven. I wanted to be like many other little innocent girls—caring, loving people, lots of friends, spending my days watching TV, riding bikes, and going to the movies. But the way my life was set up was different. I was judged and horribly misunderstood. I wasn't subject to any of these things. I was a little dark girl with nappy puff ponytails and buck teeth who was always trying to keep a smile. What a picture! I was a broken child with a lot of secrets deeper than the eyes can see.

As the years went on, I ran from pain. It was a hard transition because I realized that I was in a dysfunctional family with no love. No ever said I love you! My childhood was not the best because of the circumstances with my stepfather, who was supposed to be a protector, not a predator. He never liked me! It was crazy to me that everyone in the house acted like what was going on was normal.

Every morning, I had to go outside and not come back in until dark. If I came back in before time, I got a whooping from my stepdad, Rodney. If I said the wrong thing, I got a whooping from my stepdad, Rodney. I never felt like I was a part of the family. My siblings weren't treated the same way.

At 12 years old. I was a typical teenager, or so I thought. I was blooming, clear-faced, long pressed hair, and as they say, "smelling myself." I noticed that the aggression in stepdad's growing more and more. I was trying to stay out of his way.

Let me tell you a little about him—then you'll be able to follow me. Rodney was mean as a pit-bull, talked crazy to me and anyone else around, was very degrading to women and children and treated my mom like a dog. He hated other races and very aggressive, verbal and mentally abusive, and manipulative. He made my mom cry all the time, calling her names and always letting everyone in the house that he was in control.

At the time, I had a friend named Sharon, who I told what was going on. She replied, "Girl, he may have voodooed her." She told me to check the windows and asked was if my mom was sick whenever she came out of the front door. A question I thought was weird... But I asked her, and she replied no.

Rodney would work all week, go out on weekends, and drink and meet other women. Most nights, he would come home, and he and my mother would fight. She would throw things to destroy the house. I was in my room in my bed hearing noises made throughout the house. I lay there because, at that time, you didn't get up and speak unless spoken to. In some incidents, you shut up altogether. And then, they would "make up" and the whole house knew they were having sex! Back then, it was what it was. There weren't any boundaries when it came to that. Nobody was saying, "What about the children hearing us?" They continued like no one was there. People be more compassionate with your children in the home there young and impressionable it's not for them him to hear or see what grown-ups do!

One night, he came home late, drunk again. I saw a shadow standing at the door. My head peeped out, scared and wondering, "What is he about to do? Where he is going?" He walked over and put his hand under the covers. I was trying to stay still while he was literally pulling my legs apart. He jabbed his hand between my legs, and I screamed. When I jumped up, he ran out. My mom came and I began explaining what happened. He denied it and said that I was a troublemaker and a liar and said, "A child like that can't stay in my house!" WOW!

She believed him and that changed my life forever. When a child speaks to you, do you hear them? As things progressed, I started getting more beatings because now my mom was working, leaving us there. So, I would rebel by talking back and not wanting him to touch me or say anything to me. They were fighting more, and I was getting more and more beatings—not only from him but from her too now. Plus, my siblings and I were fighting as well.

I'm now saying, "What did I do so bad to get treated like this?" Then it happened. One day I came home, my bags were packed, and I was told that I'm going to stay with my aunt.

♦TRUST ISSUES♦

Now, my aunt Margret was a doll. I loved her but, I had never stayed with her. The transition wasn't hard, but my learning to deal with my cousins was incredibly difficult. Me wanting love from my mom now placed somewhere I didn't want to be. Now I'm with my cousins, Katherine, Patrick, and Terian and my uncle was nice, too. Katherine and I started good. I'm 14 at Chickasaw Middle School, where I joined the basketball team and met a lot of new people. I met a girl named Fe-Fe and we became inseparable. My ace boon coon, my aunt liked her a lot.

Now, I'm playing basketball, get out more, have lots of friends, and have a boyfriend. He had a twin. Everything, I believed, is going well. Then, here we go... my cousin Katherine and I started arguing and fighting all the time and about any and everything. I believe it was jealousy because she just didn't want me there, but she loved me like her sister. I had so much anger that I couldn't love her back.

Trust issues had my mind cloudy and confused. I was very defiant and manipulative. Y'all know that, as young teens, the focus is on the weakness in that they can't identify themselves. Also, teenagers can be guilt mongers. What you do to make others feel unbalanced when you know all the time that the facts are not true... Think about this! Who has been in your personal space? Were you removed from your home and it wasn't your fault? Who's told you that you will never amount to anything, you're worthless, or NOBODY wants you? Teens often feel unworthy of love and nobody listens to what they have to say! I believe we all have a voice.

When we were coming up, we were taught that, "What happens in this house stays in this house!" So, I understood why my cousin felt like she did. Before I came, she was the only girl and I came into her comfort zone. Then I started rebelling because I received unconditional love. I was sick and tired of that, so I started going to school Knowing that I could use my body to get what I wanted so I messed with my basketball coach because I had it like that! One day, I came home on the back of his motorcycle and my Aunt hit the roof! She said, "I had been looking for you all day You weren't at school, you weren't in the neighborhood but you leaving the house having sex and talking mess." Y'all she beat the brakes off me! Ask me did I stop? Noooooo!

I'm thinking that I'm popular until this girl said, "No, Sweetie, you just a HOE!" WOW!

I quickly replied, "You just mad cause I was with your man too." So, then there was a fight and I got suspended for three days. In those three days, when my cousins got up, I did too. I acted like I was going to school, but they would go in and I would just keep going.

Then, I met this dude named James. We would drink, smoke, and then... guess what's next. I would be back at school by two o'clock to walk home with my cousins, and they never knew anything. As this prolonged, I was always in trouble, doing what I want. My aunt was so understanding. She talked to me all the time. The more she talked, the angrier I would get. While being in her house, I was kissed in the mouth and attacked by a stranger. The way I saw it was that, if no one wanted me, I had no purpose in life.

Therefore, it made me angry because I'm feeling like there was a magnet attached to my head that said, "She's no good! Get her!" I coped with my anger by using sex as a weapon. I believed that would make me feel better. Behind all of that, I caught a disease, which made me have to tell my aunt what I was doing. I was taken to the health department, where I found out that I had crabs. Everyone was tired of the drama. When I returned, my bags were packed AGAIN. I'm like, "Where am I going?" No one would answer. Now I was back to where I started.

Love is an emotion that we all feel. No one deserves to be touched, beaten, strangled, lied on, lied to, made to think suicidal thoughts, or deal with mom's rejection, and dad's molestation!

I'm back in Mississippi now. I was 16 years old and in the 11th grade. I now attend Southaven High School, where I'm taking all the basic classes and also childcare.

I was in love with my teacher. She was a doll and she adored me. She taught me how to take care of a child. I learned what to do if the child is crying, how to change a diaper, etc. This made me feel lonely, so I wanted a baby. I was like WOW!

When a teenager feels like they're not getting love at home, you question God. Then, you say, "Why not have a baby? You know for a fact that he or she will love you!" With that in mind, I started hanging out in our small town. They had juke joints on the square, which was the spot on Fridays and Saturdays. THE WEST END! Tanya, Brea, and I were in that thang, spiraling out of control.

Knowing that we were everything that most people couldn't be or wanted to be-- money, hot girls, and the center attraction—that was the party spot for the town. Everybody knew everybody, so there was never a dull moment. I met a 28-year-old guy named Melvin and we got acquainted. We started hanging out and my mom would drop me off and tell me it's okay. When she asked me, "What y'all be doing?" I would say, "We have so much fun!"

I never got the story of the birds and the bees. People talk to your children! Don't let Social media grow them up, unlike me, the streets taught me. See I wasn't told that your cookie is the most precious thing you have! I'm doing what I think I know because I thought he loved me. I remember a time when my mom called to pick me up and his mom told her, "Oh, they're in the back having sex!" Then I had the nerve to be mad like what did she think we were doing! Still, I was taken to the doctor. I got a whooping and they had this thing where my stepdad loved for me to get straddle the chair and my mom would say, "Take everything off and lay down!" As I look back now, that was his means of being aroused but she never saw that. It wasn't right because I was the only one that got that kind of abuse.

As they did before, they moved on and never said anything else about it! I'm out having mad relations and then POP... I'm three months pregnant, wondering how I am going to tell my mom and stepdad. Well, I wasn't showing, but somehow, my mom knew, and I was hit and pushed. I remember falling down steps, but I wasn't hurt. She was angry and my stepdad wanted me to either move out or get rid of it. Believe it or not, I talked to Melvin and he was excited. I was happy but unsure because of how crazy my living situation is.

My mom got excited, but my stepdad looked like he was getting angrier. He showed a look of disgust. I was terrified of him because of all the cursing and yelling all the time. Sometimes it was unbearable all I wanted was peace.

Soon, I was tired of being pregnant. I'm in my ninth month and a friend of mine said, "Barbara, get in a whirlpool. It will make the baby come down quicker." That didn't work, so then the next attempt was having sex. She told me that it would make me go into labor. Ladies, that doesn't work either.

Well, my bundle of joy came in her own time, and it was love. My child made me feel complete. I felt like I was loved. She bought enjoyment in my life and inside my house. There was less attention on me and more to my angel, Tamara. Her dad was there from the time she turned one until she turned five. After that, I was on my own again, taking care of her and starting our lives.

I needed to figure out how I was going to take care of us. I had a revelation, telling me to, "Do something with your life because nothing will be handed to you on a silver platter." My favorite quote is this, "You don't work, you don't eat."

♦THAT TIME AT HAIR SCHOOL...♦

I'm now 17 years old in the twelfth-grade thinking, "I'm going to have a great year. I'm graduating, finishing hair school, yes, hair school. I'm 17 and got it going on." I was enrolled at 16 and I'm also enrolled at the IBA School of Cosmetology. Mrs. Payne was the best instructor and taught me how to curl short hair. Ms. Penny taught me all the attitude and how to relate to the clients. Ms. Faye taught me personal finance and how to make money. She was a true money maker with goals and ambition.

People say I have the "gift of gab", meaning that I know how to talk a good game, set out, and do whatever it takes. I was the top of my class, the girl everybody looked up to. They thought had all the answers! I was Miss IBA, won all the hair shows, and mastered those curling irons. So, I knew I would have a future, taking care of me and my baby girl.

One day a lady my aunt knew came into IBA. When you enter a hair school, you sign a waiver stating that the school is not responsible for anything that happens to your hair.

She came in and said, "I want a relaxer." I went to our dispensary. This where they assigned students to work for a day and sometimes a week to learn products. Gabrielle handed me what I thought was relaxer and she assumed it was as well. I went to drape and base her. I gloved up the fourth part and I am now applying the relaxer. All of a sudden, the teacher walked by.

"Barbara, what's that?"

I said, "Relaxer."

She said, "It smells awfully strong!"

I told her, "Gabrielle gave it to me." She went over to the dispensary to check it was Thioglycolate, which was used for Jheri curls back in the day. We took her to the shampoo bowl, rinsed out her hair, and it was sliding off her scalp as the water hit it! We stopped. Ms. Faye ran and got some 911 Emergency to stop the breakage. It stopped shedding and she had peach fuzz on her head. When she sat up, it was devastating! She was crying and hollering, and I was too. I calmed down, but the floor was out of control. She calmed down, too, and we started putting things in order. We convinced Alana to cut her hair short with a nice line and she liked it. She came back after that and, over the years, I've seen her and there are no hard feelings, thank God!

Fast forward-- I've graduated from Southaven High School by a landslide! After hair school, I went to work for this lady named Jesse who had opened a hair salon. I worked in the salon in Hernando for a while, meeting great people. Lucy Reed was a great stylist and experienced with wet set hairstyles. I was a Marcel curler and Jessie was an all-around stylist. and Larry was the finger wave king. We all could learn from each other.

I wanted more and more growth, which led me to move to Memphis. Before I left, we had a scheduled out of town hair show. I'm single and the only one going without a mate.

We get to Florida. It's hot too—the back of my legs and my face were on fire from the heat hitting me so hard! I didn't know what to do.

We went sight-seeing and the city was beautiful! We ate in some of the finest restaurants. I loved Disney World—the rides, people, and all the attractions—but I saved the best for last. The hair show was an excellent experience. It was a blast, but all these people were much older than me and they were like my parents! It was always, "don't do this, leave that alone, don't talk to them."

I had to be with them for five days. We were on day three and now, I'm getting pissed. I tell them that I paid my money just like everybody else and I'm grown. They told me that I was in their care, so deal with it. Jessie had all tickets back.

I'm young, but still smart! I told her that was fine. Now, everybody has an attitude with me, not answering when I ask a question. I snapped because they were making me have flashbacks of home. I called the bus station bought a ticket, called a cab, and the next morning as everybody was eating, I said goodbye. I left them in Florida, made it back to Mississippi, packed up my things from the salon, and went home.

◆LIVIN' LIFE LAVISH◆

Shortly after returning from Florida, I moved out of my mother's house because I was told that all grown people needed their own house. I went and got my apartment at the Mill Creek Apartments. I was a kitchen beautician, doing hair at home. I made money, the clientele was booming, and it was crazy! I did so much hair that I would have to come out of my back door instead of the front because someone was always waiting for me. The biggest thing I remember about that experience was this: I had a can I used to save my money in, and, to this day, I still use it. It's for change now, but I bank it up—times have changed!!!

After I moved in, my friend named Theresa moved in with me. We were clubbing it big! I'm 18 and she's 19. I'm working at Rube La Lynda, where the owners gave me a chance even when I didn't have a client. When you leave the salon house, the clients don't follow. The game changed because I can't come when I wanted to and prices changed, so I still had to pay booth rent—that jar money came in handy.

At first, I was in the back working then I requested to be upfront so I could see the walk-ins when they walked in. They did put me up front and placed be beside a woman who was an angel to me and I'm going to tell you why!

Tamela was one of the best hairstylists in Memphis, TN. She and her sister Naomi were extremely nice and encouraged me. Tamela gave me clients to serve and helped me build my clientele to where I am today. I will always respect and appreciate her for that!

As I grew, there were many obstacles put in my way. My friend Tiny wanted to work at the salon, so I enrolled her in hair school. I took her some days and my boyfriend every day took her when I couldn't. This went on until she was able to buy a car. She bought a new blue Geo Prism—how exciting for her. She received her license and then we started working together. We even went out together and now it's me, Angel, Sarah, Tanji, and Tiny! We are all out there, young and very impressionable. One fun experience we had together was FreakNik.

We all got tattoos. Mine was on my stomach. It was a tiger jumping over a waterfall. Sarah got two tiger prints on her breast. When pushed together, they say, "Watch out." Angel's tattoo was on her left thigh—the eye of the tiger. When she wears her short dresses or shorts, you can see it. Tanji's tattoo was on her left breast—a beautiful red rose like her.

We went to the ATL four cars deep with our other friends. When we arrived, it was still night, going into the early morning. We walked the strip, ate breakfast, then we checked in to our hotel.

What an experience! People were having sex in the hallways, on the couches in the lobby, and the elevators—everywhere!

We all changed clothes. Tiny was trying to sell Sarah to the next highest guy and she wasn't going! Tiny gave everybody some Coochie Coupons; these were for every guy we wanted to sleep with. As you can tell, Tiny was the leader and we all listened to her. She said, "I'm not going to mess with everybody... just guys with money."

One time, we were at the restaurant eating and a guy was coming on to her. He had several other friends with him, all talking and laughing, having fun. Tiny and the guy started talking mess and, before we knew it, she was in a booth with her legs up in the air letting him do her! As it came to an end; she quoted our favorite saying, "Coochie Coupon Check 1." Hours later, we went down to the beach where we were all on the prowl looking for freaks. They all found good potential and decided that it was time to use our Coochie Coupons once again. A couple of us decided to chill on the beach and take pictures of several fine-looking dudes.

Tiny, the shit talker, decided to take a guy up to the room to drink and kick it. The other girls were working, making their money, and handling business.

As we go into our next phase, my girl Nicky D proved to be a true money maker. She loved money, men, and clothes. As we would all put on our clothes the next day, Nicki D looked to see if somebody out dressed her. If they did, she would change her clothes. She laid out and threw on clothes until she felt like she was top notch. Nicki D and Tiny used to get into it all the time because Nicki D used to bring dudes to the door without confirming it with Tiny. Therefore, Tiny couldn't take the fact that Nicki D wouldn't jump to her command—it used to drive her insane.

Have you ever heard the saying, "Monkey see, monkey do?" Well, this situation was the total opposite, Tiny figured because everybody else followed her that Nicki D would come aboard. Nicki D told her that she was a leader, not a follower so it was like a volcano exploding. Yes, we were followers and I felt like I needed that direction. Tiny knew she couldn't compete, but a challenge is what she liked. My girl got so mad that she left the FreakNik headed back to Memphis because she was sick of it. We saw her off and continued with the fun.

As the day went into the night, I got back up to the room and they are kicking it, dinking some Kristal, talking about everything, and smoking weed. Tiny had the nerve to start having sex like I'm not in the room. I came out of the bathroom like really and had the nerve to look at me and continue! She had the "What's up" look. I got my stuff and zoomed out of there.

As the trip proceeds on, a lot of things happened. I can't say I regret anything because we were young people who loved to party and knew how to kick it without robbing, stealing, or killing to get by.

Headed back home, everybody was tired. we stopped to gas up the cars and people are still following us. We pull out the gas station going the wrong way in oncoming traffic. Who was driving? Tiny! We had a terrible accident! The driver in one car was hurt and rushed to the hospital, the car behind us totaled and, when the police arrived, tickets were given. This girl's insurance was so good they sent another rental car so we could get on to the house. We get to the M town and work began all over again I'm feeling myself because I've had a great trip! My attitude was way up there and I'm saying, "I'm never going to change me!"

I had a double personality. Barbara is sweet, loving, loves people, and loves to explore new things. Then you have Brenda, who is outgoing, but personal and somewhat of an aggressor. She gives orders, means what she says, and is always to be taken seriously.

I have to pray at times because when the spirit jumps on you... Lord, I don't know if all that I do is always right, but I know I don't do a lot of wrongs. I'm a good person—I love and try to help everyone when I can.

My life is so complicated! I'm unhappy at times, but I have examined myself. Trying and trying to please others is a curse. The more I pray about it, it gets better, but I still fall back. As they say, take two steps up and something or somebody will make you take four back. My trusting skills are set up like this, "I see you, but I'm always watching and never listening to what you tell me." I don't know when to believe and when not to. A lot of times I believe things I shouldn't. I trust what people say and I probably shouldn't. I ask you, Lord, to please help me to understand... my heart is crumbling, and my soul is aching. I believe you shall not fight stone for stone, but I do believe that if you do wrong, wrong will follow. The scripture I learned says, "No weapons formed against me shall prosper." But what I had to realize is that the people I keep let doing me in keep prospering and I so don't understand. HELP ME LORD TO UNDERSTAND how and why! I need clarity... Matthew 7 says, "Ask and it shall be given to you."

♦MIRROR ON THE WALL♦

My journey continues...

Although I was feeling this way, I had to find a way to work out my problems. As I continue, I'm 20 and haven't experienced life like most young people, but always thought I was grown. I'm out here running with my buddies that were everywhere—clubs, parties, etc.—and had plenty of boyfriends. I was going out all the time to this one club, CLUB NO NAME, which always stood out to me.

"All the pretty girls have a seat in the front and All the ugly girls please stand up in the back."

I was live. I loved it. Mingling, dancing, and hanging out, doing my thing—I was on a prowl for somebody's attention. I was a dresser, I thought! I wore tight pants, a fly off the shoulder shirt—my signature STAMPED! That's the grown and sexy part of me—my six-inch heels, flashy jewelry (you know how we do it), and my long straight twelve-inch weave. I would put myself to shame I'm so HOTTTTT!

This was how I saw life... I felt like a mirror on the wall. You know how you look at yourself and see one thing, but someone else looks at you and sees a whole different person? People saw me but formed what they wanted me to be. I didn't love myself so how could I love others. My three abusers labeled me, so those were the things I thought were true about me. I was always told things like, "Girl, you're great at what you do in bed." So, I decided to use sex at a weapon to make me fill that void from the pain. It was my self-medication. At the time, that was the best pain reliever.

In my relationships, it was what they wanted me to be. My first abuser said that I would be nothing without him. With my second abuser, I was only good for things like helping him make money My third abuser said that no one wanted me but him. During all this, I was what you called a Dope Man's $itch.

15

I was the ride or die chick. Thinking back now, I scare myself when I think about how God spared my life through me being robbed at the salon and at home, getting shot at rolling under cars, fighting for my life, car jacketed, and picking up dope money. My God! Of course, I thought that was love because no one ever showed me or taught me anything different; therefore, I was seeking attention and they said those famous words, "I LOVE YOU!"

Here we go...

I was in the club one night when this guy named Antonio approached me. He was the friend of my friend Bridgette, who was dating Tank. Now Tank is what you call a smooth operator—got a woman at the house and women in the streets. He always had his business together. Both women knew about each other, parted together, socialized at church, and with each other at times. Not because they wanted to, but because they had to. After all, he was the man for real and they both knew that. They say pimping ain't easy, but in this case, yes it was! Let's move on back to Antonio.

Bridgette said, "Girl, get that money!" He was a hot boy by night and hard worker by day. Like that famous quote says, "Good girls like bad boys." This story has a twist, though! He slept all day, got up mid evenings and ate, drank hung out with his friends, smoked weed, and sold drugs all night. I was so misconstrued.

I entered the relationship thinking, "He'll be nice to me treat me right. Keep me FRESH!!!!!!! Love me the way I need to be loved." So, I proceed on with him. Days went on to months, months went on to a year, so it was great!!

Soon, it took a turn for the worst. I found out he was the top dope man, driving a white Cadillac truck and hanging with The Who's Who in the M-town. He took me on shopping sprees.

Who am I... stupid? I liked to get slapped. I had a man who liked to beat on me, degrade me in front of others, and beat me in secluded areas, yet he pleased me with unforgettable pleasures.

I was at the relationship point of no return. He started dictating orders like, "Put my clothes in the cleaners... needed to be out by 5. You hear me?" Okay... there I go I can do that. Then, "You better be in before ten o'clock!" I felt I was still in high school, but then, I did that! Keep in mind that I'm working a lot of hours at the salon. Because of him, I'm taking clients and rushing cause I felt like I had to do this. I saw my relationship becoming just like my mom's relationship. I had experienced so much trauma for so long. I grew up watching my mom take orders and be told what to do. That made me think it was normal. I got really pissed off when he got on my friends. All of a sudden it was, "You can't hang out with Bridgette on the weekends anymore. Fix their hair cause its money, but that's it!"

The red flag came up I'm telling him, "I've grown up with them! My friends are family to me. Why I can't socialize with them?" You would have thought the military set a missile! This nigga exploded! He hit me so hard my body shifted. I had a crook in my neck, my hip felt like it shifted, and when I hit the floor, this trick kicked me in the back! It was an unbelievable thing—like I was having a nightmare while I was awake! I know you're saying, "She stupid! What was wrong with her? Why she didn't leave?"

I'm going to tell you why...

When you've been abused, what we know is wrong looks right. That's all you know at the time. Take heed... I'm young, saying that he didn't mean it because, after he did it, we made passionate love. Afterward, he got up and fixed something to eat.

When he realized I wasn't going anywhere, the beatings were more frequent. I felt like I never had time to heal. After a while, I decided to leave for a while and went down to my mom's house. I was still in turmoil then I went back to him because I couldn't take my stepdad picking on me just because he could. He knew I was scared of him and I knew he would either try me or put me in the streets. He was mentally abusing my mom, so I couldn't take all the burdens and cursing every evening when getting off work. It was very nerve-wracking.

I didn't want to be there, either. I'm stuck between a rock and a hard place. Take a minute to think about this... This wasn't my first domestic violence issue! I've already been molested and verbally abuses as a child, so I'm looking for that male role model to fill the void of being daddy—something or someone. I've never had the pleasure of having a father figure. So, to the men who are reading this, Daddies, tell your girls they are beautiful! You're their protectors They need to hear, "I'll be with you through the good and bad" and that their cookie is the most precious gift that they have, so save it till marriage. Speak life into your children and seek growth within your relationships with your daughters.

Take your baby girl aside and let them know that you love them, are there to motivate them, you care for them, you want to know everything about them, and keep up with them. Daddies, tell your young men to wrap it up cause sticking it in the wrong places can get them a bundle of joy for 18 years or something they can't get rid of. I'm talking about these babies you may not be ready for and don't bring that baby here to suffer cause a child doesn't ask for that. If a young girl tells you, "Don't worry", don't believe it! You keep it moving. I say wait if you can.

As we return to the story, I'm back at Antonio's house because I felt like a visitor—never home sweet home for me. There was one situation when he was mad that I was out with Bridgette at Club Orchard downtown. You go in at night and, when you come out, it's morning.

"Wow! Man, I didn't know we partied all night." When I arrived home wanting to explain, I was locked out of my room and had to sleep on the couch. Next thing I know a girl was coming out, passing me, and telling me good morning! She acted like she stayed there, and I was the visitor. Man, I jumped up to him choking me, slapping me around, and then raping me over and over. Now you're saying, "How is it that? Cause it's one thing to give it to them and another thing to take it!" I knew that, if I didn't, the beating would continue. I was so terrified I was not allowed to leave the house, talk on the phone, or go into work. After a while, we made up and I'm out of the house feeling free, but he still was checking on me at the shop and monitoring my calls—crazy him or crazy me?

The straw that broke the camel's back was when I lost some customers at the shop. After that, I decided to get a part-time job at the Nike factory on Shelby Drive. I loved working there, but the shift was six PM to six AM. When I went to work, it was dark and it was morning when I got off. But anyway, I left work for one day and Antonio decides he wants to have a day party. Dudes and girls were everywhere! I came into a full-fledged orgy. I make it to my bedroom and saw two girls doing each other and he was doing some girl himself. So, I'm screaming, telling them to get out—he closed the door and LOCKED IT! I sat in my car looking like a fool, waiting until it was over.

We didn't say anything to each other because, by then, I knew I was in a bad place. I'm selling my soul to the devil because, when we went to sleep later that night, one of the girls must have come back or never left. His cousin, who was his roommate, got up and went to the other room. I hear all kinds of noises and, when the noise finally stops, I questioned him about it. He explodes and beats me till he was tired. That next morning when he left, I packed everything my little blue Chevette could hold. Now I'm headed to Mississippi to get my daughter and bring her up here to the city with me.

When I left, a restraining order was put on him and he was told never to contact me again. Back then, the law was that! The men or women understood, but now, these violet offenders do not understand restraining orders. If they say, "I'm going to get you," they're coming without any remorse! They don't respect the authority of the law, so what makes you different. No matter how far you go down the wrong road, you can always turn back.

Once I left his house, I got another apartment in the Southwyck Apartments on Shelby Drive across from the Southland Mall. Man, what a great time for me! I'm living life and loving it. I was doing hair at the house because I lost a lot of clients at the salon. I was doing hair in both places, still trying to maintain. One bright sunny day, I was feeling a little distorted about my relationship as well as life. So, I should have been out there riding in my shiny red convertible vet, but instead of that, I called a dear friend, an older elder lady named Ms. Aretha. She was one of the sweetest, reliable, and courteous women you ever wanted to meet. She said, "Baby, when you get tired of all the foolishness around you, then only you will know. So, stand up to your potential because you are great. Now show it." I started traveling to Atlanta, Detroit, Chicago, Alabama, and Texas to pursue my career in platform artistry.

As time flies, I sat around all these other artists with confidence, feeling like I wasn't worthy or strong enough, so I came back home and settled for what I had. I wasn't mentally ready for all the excitement and limelight that came with working with others. I fell short because, for a person to conquer what they set out to do, they need courage, strength, and guidance. I needed self-esteem, which I didn't have, to be around others of that caliber. Therefore, I was out of my comfort zone, which was behind the chair doing hair, so that's why I ran like a chicken with my head cut off, scared of change.

I kept myself busy at the salon. I was back to making good money because clients were coming in regularly. I had an extremely beautiful house in Germantown that was newly remodeled with a beautiful wood finish, and a paint job that was out of this world. Every room custom made furniture carved from beautiful cherry wood. The window trim for the hanging of my blinds was ordered –they were so nice. At this moment, I felt like I was living well.

Now, let me tell you how I got my car. I went on the Gossett lot over on Mt Moriah just to look around, not intending to buy a car. At this moment, I had a Ford Explorer that was paid for, but I saw this pearl white Lexus with a grey bottom. I talked to the salesman, telling my situation. He convinced me to file the paperwork and I did. Before I knew it, I asked Karen to come to pick my truck up because I was about to ride away in my brand new car. What a beautiful sight—a white Lexus for a Black queen. I'm looking for a change, so my baby and I were just living.

As for my daughter, Michella—young, innocent, very sweet, and had a bubbly personality! She was Mommy's little princess and I gave her whatever she wanted... It's on and popping I feel that I got my life back! Then this guy named George approached me the salon one day, playing about some scissors he thought I had from his barber Calvin. He seemed to be a nice guy at first. He took me out to some of the finest restaurants, had me picked up in a limousine for dinner on several occasions. When we were out, he showered me with the finer things in life—things a woman deserved—and bought me whatever I wanted as well as needed. He took me in and out of town, always made sure I had money, and I felt safe and protected with him.

◆BLIND TO THE SIGNS◆

Now, let me now give you a little history on him. I found the truth out later down the line—six months into the relationship. George was a street player. He was my "Gorilla Pimp," my favorite song at the time:

Talking to pimp you done broke the first rule
Imma come on your job imma act a fool
If anyone step in our biz imma slap them too
All that loud talking girl you can gone settle down
For your friend have to pick you up off the ground

Women see the signs! We hear what's being said but, when you think you're in love, nothing matters ...

They called him Mr. Tulane because he ran his mouth all the time and stayed in other people's business like he was a god. He thought he was Mr. Untouchable—NOT! He stayed getting beat up! He talked a mighty bluff but was soft as tissue, weak as water—only to a nigga, though not to women. He would be a women's worst nightmare.

When he approached me, all I saw was his smooth caramel skin and how he was very well-groomed, always dressed fresh, and always smelled good. Now behind all that I was still blind with that money, money, and more money. Now, the red flags are already up. What should I DO? LEAVE HIM ALONE OR CONTINUE? What do you think I did? Soon, I'm two months pregnant, preparing for my son.

George has slapped me on some occasions, but he had since started beating me. The beatings got worse when he caught me cheating on him with another dope boy named Ali, who he had beef with in the street. Oh, how I loved him so, but I knew when I got caught that I couldn't have them both anymore. Now I've been physically abused in public, with knocking my teeth out. He had me robbed at the salon because he had beef with someone I used to work with. It was officially funny because the day

21

before, they got into it and the next day, she didn't come to work. He hit my car, I hit his side piece's car and he ran off the road into a ditch.

Another incident happened where he came to the salon, got mad at me, and ran me out of the salon because I wouldn't give him any money. He chased me through the woods and beat me up. Now I'm sure it seems that I could have stopped at any time, but I thought if he didn't hit me, he didn't love me. So many women think this way! Love isn't supposed to hurt. Do what I decided after all of this—get my car back from him that he was driving! Yes, ladies! I bought him a brand-new Blue Cadillac!

One night, I followed him and watched him and a girl go into her house. I got the car pulled! My friend Bridgette taught me how to track a man down, so I did that! Oh, did I know he would stalk me! I moved out of the apartment, but he came to the salon and threatened everyone, so I stood my ground because I wasn't going to let him keep that car. I moved out of the salon, gave him the car back, and then had the car lot go get it. Next, I got an order of protection—then he realized I wasn't playing with him, so he finally moved on. As I moved on, I'm finally a licensed cosmetologist and now, it's all about me, my kids, and my career.

In soul searching, this trait characteristic evolved to objectify the structure of personality. According to Freud's Theory, the perspective about a person with low self-esteem is when there are made aware that it has to be addressed and brought to the surface so that they can receive the help that's needed. Low self-esteem brings on depression, a lack of responsibility toward others and, a lack of positive self-image. A person has to believe in themselves before others believe in them. In describing the perspective, a teenager in my culture back in the day is different from teenagers now. They have to learn to have a mind of their own. However, a lesson to be administered is to learn to be a leader instead of a follower. Beauty is in the eye of the beholder and you never let anyone tear down your self-esteem. The assumption is that, the more a person is lowered and talked about, the stronger it makes them. No one has the right to bring another person down. Everyone lives in the same world dominated by mass media. Everyone is going to be beautiful. People should not allow other people to lower their confidence, make them feel second rate, or criticize them. Just learn to love the person inside and, without a doubt, happiness will come.

Years later, I met a guy named Tyron When meeting him, I thought he was my knight in shining armor. He said the right things and knew how to please me in every way. Now, his tone at times bothered me, but I'd had worse, so I just turned the other cheek because I figured I would help him with his anger. As the relationship grew, I started letting him bring me lunch at the salon Angelica's on Winchester. I had great clientele!

One day, a lady called to get her hair done. I was open she came by and

Tyron brought me some food. Tell me why not only the lady knew him, but also knew he had a baby the same age as my son Greg. Well, that day I found out that whatever looks good to you is not necessarily good for you!

My life shifted again. Right after I let that wall down, his baby momma called me to talk. She let me know that they were not together for all kinds of reasons—they used to fight all the time, they couldn't see eye to eye about anything, and she wanted to make sure I knew she didn't want him back! She just wanted him to take care of his son—well, we did just that. His son was the sweetest baby! When the second baby momma popped up, I ended up with Mesha, Greg, Barron, and William at my house every weekend. Oh, how I felt like we had a ready-made family! He loved me, the children, and both baby mommas, Regina and Tasha.

But as life continued, Tyron started getting jealous because I was spending time with Regina. Things started getting physical because he couldn't and wouldn't approve of us being friends. After a while, the abuse had gotten so bad that he chased me out of my house with my daughter there. She's upset and running behind me. At the time, Greg was over to his grandma's house. I told him it was over!

After I moved on, he started stalking me. One night, he came over because I had another male company. He came through a window to let me know he was the boss of that house. I told the guy he had to go. Even through all of this, I still loved him! Here we go again—this time, I made it clear because he'd jumped on me over my friend Lydia s house! Enough is Enough! From there, I went on to do what I knew to do—make me some money.

♦MY SO CALLED SILENT LIFE♦

I was accustomed to having nice things and I knew I had the brains and Regina had the body, so she was a stripper with lots of talents. She had this one trick that made us thousands and thousands of dollars! The girl was so bad! She would take ten huge balls, insert them into her private parts, and pull them out one by one—from smallest to biggest then you heard the POP!! Men used to go crazy and throw money and book plenty of parties. Now I'm moving and my business is growing

Later, I met this guy named Richard in Mississippi and he introduced me to another whole level of life. Every weekend, I started bringing women to this club I formed called Ebony Illusion. We had a club secluded for all types of fun. I had a full staff and my girl Saddie took the money at my door. I would sell tickets and have a bus to pick people up in Memphis, drive them to Mississippi, and drop them back off after the party. I thought I was living the good life—little did I know that, even though I left my abuser, I was manipulating others to do what I had in my mind and wanted them to do. I didn't see why I needed anyone at this point, I believed I was the head woman in charge!

As I finish this chapter in my life, I decided that I was going to move in silence. When you almost get tied up with a do or die situation, it's time to move forward! Pimping ain't easy, but sooner or later, someone will pay the price. Me? I liked my freedom, so it was time to stop!

Don't let someone who mistreats you make you think that there's something wrong with you. Don't devalue yourself because they didn't value you! Know your worth, even if they don't! Period...

I tried all I could do to move forward to bigger and better things, but I kept reverting to my old ways. At 43, through all these things, I'm still seeking love and always running into negative things and people. I was working in my salon, B Love B Beautiful Hair Salon, "Hair Care for the Classy Woman". I was going to church every Sunday, singing on the praise team, working as a lady of the night, being a sexual manipulator, and even being a swinger in and out of town. Then that call came— "You've caught a sexually transmitted disease!" Y'all I had gonorrhea, trigeminal, and even got crabs again! I knew these things I did were wrong, but when you're so lonely and looking to fill a void, it's hard to see what others see. At this point in my life, I know that I'm a vessel for others because God had my back and knew my pain.

♦MY VOID TO FILL♦

In 1997, I met the sweetest young lady, who attended Wooddale Middle School. She contacted me because she was looking for a hairstylist for her eighth-grade prom. Some friends of hers were already my clients, so she decided to make her a hair appointment with me at the famous BLoveBBeautiful Hair Salon.

The moment this girl got into my chair, our bond began. She automatically started telling me stories about her childhood. As people know, your hairstylist is your counselor and therapist. So, I shared my childhood of my auntie raising me and how I didn't feel like I had a mother figure in my life. Also, the streets raised made me grow up fast.

From that day on, I started doing her hair from eighth grade until. She gained a bond with my son and daughter and, as years went by, she even started to babysit them in her high school days. She had a baby at the age of 19. I loved that baby just like she was my flesh and blood—I love her now. I treated her like she's my granddaughter. I tried my best to teach her how to be a great mother also and taught her how to be a young woman. She saw my work ethic in the salon and learned what I had to do to take care of my kids. She learned how she was supposed to take care of her baby as a young mother. She watched me raise so many kids in her adult life and I'm so glad that I could be a great inspiration in my life and so many others!

Everyone doesn't have that mom or dad in their home life. Whether they're present or not, a parent's love, approval, or time is very important! A message to my parents: Work toward making a mark on your children's lives by being there for them through the good and the bad! We fight for that missing piece of the pie, which sometimes causes us to make poor judgments. Pay attention to your children!

I found myself in a place where I needed something to fill a void—still looking for love to validate me. I started a majorette team called the

Dynamic Dymonds, where my goal was to give love to girls who were seeking to make a difference.

Also, they were looking in all the wrong places for their salon. So, as this journey continued, my girls were elementary, middle, and high school girls. Hamilton, Gaston, McFarland, Whitehaven, and Pine Hill Community Centers were my stomping grounds. Tamara, Harrietta, Tonya, CeCe Ellan, Paula, Miche, Diana, Niya, Angel, Tiny were my kids who always stood out.

CeCe, Tamara, Tonya, Harrietta, Angela, Paula were my ride or die girls. Those were my "I don't play about Ms. B and when we dance, we dance out of the love from our heart."

For instance, I remember when we were practicing at Pine Hill. The girls were minding their own business and these girls were constantly bothering them. Honey, my kids told me, "Ms. B, they won't stop talking about us." The girls continued with the night and when we walked out of the building, the girls jumped them! I'm still not into fighting and I taught my kids not to start a confrontation, but at this time, they were stuck together. I got the girls off them, pinned them down, and called police. I got the director and the girls were banned from ever returning to the community center.

On that night, I realized my child Harrietta always had a razor under her tongue, and by me always preaching to her and my wild child, she asked no questions. That night, I had to deal with that before she hurt herself or somebody. As we moved on, these young ladies—are now grown women with lives, homes, jobs, and children—are still with my daughter. Many still call me everything from Ms. Barbara to Momma.

Speaking life into these women has helped me with all the heartaches and anger issues I had. It showed me that I had love to give that a lot of them was missing, so I declare this to all my dance choreographers, majorettes, hip hop mentors on leaders:

Throughout history, dance has been used as a spiritual expression, mating ritual, storytelling, non-verbal form of communication, and for fun. I've been a mother, sponsor, choreographer, a teacher, mentor, even a lemon squeeze facilitator. This form of a dance that you guys are experiencing, it will take you a long way in life. All you have to do is pay attention at practice, show love to your fellow team members, treat each other with respect and dignity, and this will make you well-developed, inspirational dancers with the passion to do anything you set yourself to be.

To my mentors, leaders, choreographers, teach your children:

1. Love not only themselves but also others
2. Forgiveness to whoever has hurt them so they can heal
through any circumstances
3. Trust with their whole heart! Speak life into them, not negativity (ex. You're not good enough, you're not small enough, that's why the other girls don't mess with you cause you're not on our level, make them feel all

alone in a crowded room).

    4. Sportsmanship—win or lose, we're still champions

No "you guys suck," that's your fault because you're the coach, so look at your character—that says a lot about your mentality. We are the individuals the children look up to! Let's save lives because they are our FUTURE tomorrows.

♦SICKNESS REVEALS THE REAL♦

I'm now 47 years old. After all these years, I'm just now realizing who I am and who I'm supposed to be. Of course, I know that am a woman with a purpose—to change other's lives from the inside out.

I started my new journey by first I was sick. I had been sick for years, but I always put it on stomachaches or ulcers. All the while, I had fibroids. In 2018, my whole word did another spin! I rushed to the doctor one morning with a stomachache. From there, he said it was my appendix. I drove myself to St. Francis's emergency room. After sitting there for about five minutes, I was told to come to the back. They looked at me and said, "Honey, if it was your appendix, you wouldn't have been able to walk in here." More tests were done. They don't see anything, so I left. I was still in pain, but it was bearable. Then that night—OMG—I wake up in unbearable pain. I drove out to Baptist in Collierville, just for them to them tell me I had fibroids. But then, they see a spot. A spot means it may be cancer. Also, they said no sugar because cancer feeds off that!

Now, I knew the Lord but was not really in the place where I needed to be with Him. That night, I was sick, but they had me sedated enough that I could go home. I had an appointment the next day at the West Clinic. The doctor said, "I see something and call someone because you can't leave until you do!" I called my sister, told her, and from there, we scheduled the surgery. My next appointment was when more tests were run...still no change...

I got all my business in order at home and at work. I had all the support from family and friends, GHS parents, and children. Let me tell you this— get sick and see who comes to see about you! So, the night before surgery I had a meltdown and said, "I'm going now," so Mesha called in Greg and reinforcements.

So, the big day arrives. At five AM, my sister called and was already on her way to my house to take me. She picks me up, we get there, and of course, we wait. I'm nervous! I go to the back and I'm still frantic—crying, hollering, upset, but something said to me, "You're going to be okay. Calm down."

Now, y'all may be wondering why all of this. In a minute, I'm going to tie this into what, when, how, and then why I'm still here.

As we move on, I go into surgery. It went fine. They said that my blood pressure and vitals were fine. They had to put a C bag on me because the fibroids were attached to my bladder. Now, if you have never had this, it's the worst feeling trying to use the bathroom from the other end. Also, this thing felt like it was coming out. I had to have around the clock help.

I had friends to spend the night with me. I had friends to come to cook breakfast and dinner... and even had friends to pay my rent. The beauty salon never missed a beat.

My significant other, Carlos, came up there but didn't stay. When I got discharged, he pulled up at the door and got mad cause he had to get my meds. He had somewhere else to go. Now, I'm already physically hurt. To add to that, I'm getting mentally abused because he didn't have time to deal with me now. All this time, this man had been in my corner, loved me, respected me, gave me anything I asked for even gave me a ring, and made sure the bills I ask him to pay got paid.

But you know when your man either has lost interest in you or has another woman. This left me time to think and pray for guidance and strength. All I knew was, when I got better and was able to get on my feet, the relationship was over. No one wants someone if they can't get that emotional connection.

Through healing, my friend Sasha had to pray for me. She reminded me that I was a very special person who loved hard and needed to focus on myself and learning to love me like I love others.

When it came to my last two doctors' appointments, my friend Salina took me and the doctor said, "You have healed gracefully! The bag comes out now and you closed back up well. You are cancer-free! We don't even see that spot anymore. No sign..."

I'm back up to business, but I had to stay with Carlos because I felt like he may change, or it just could have been my emotion because of the meds.

Now women, if your gut tells you something, it's true! I asked him on two different occasions if there was another woman. "No," he said.

I asked him one last time and he said, "Yes... not one, but two." He said that he didn't love them like he loved me. He wanted me to choose if I was going to say with him or not.

I let him know, "Since you're being truthful, let me tell you this, I'm precious in Someone else's eyes. He loves me for me, cherishes me, supplied all my needs, watches over me, and gives me strength. I can tell Him anything! He is my Everything like I'm His. He's my Father God Almighty. And with Him, I will be okay."

That was the last day and last encounter. That led me to speak out about sexual abuse and domestic violence with Faith Over Fear Tour Group. Now I'm growing closer to God every day.

In 2018, this group taught me love, strength, commitment, and encouraged me. Anyone who knows me knows I hated public speaking, but this group gave me the platform to be myself, worked through my kinks, prepared me for speaking, going from tablet to my paper, and speaking from the heart.

For that, I thank You cause in 2020 I've built a platform for women all over the world to stand up for yourself. Love thy enemies, love thy Neighbor and Love yourself more than anything.

To me, this Me-Too Movement is a much-needed movement in our communities today. I am glad that so many women have gained enough confidence to tell their stories and break the silence. It took me years to feel comfortable enough to tell my story. I still have to deal with certain family members being upset about me being vocal about the abuse I experienced. But breaking the silence is how we are going to end the vicious cycle of abuse.

The WHY I leave with you:

1. Have you experienced trauma in your life? If so, why are you not speaking out?

   _____

   _____

   _____

   _____

   _____

2. Are you loving your kids or are you loving the man more?

   _____

   _____

   _____

   _____

   _____

3. Could you live with the fact that you didn't listen to your child?

   _____

   _____

   _____

   _____

_____

_____

4. Are you keeping secrets?

_____

_____

_____

_____

_____

5. Can you live with knowing that you turned your back on your child?

_____

_____

_____

_____

_____

6. What's the biggest obstacle raising your confidence level?

_____

_____

_____

_____

_____

7. What different can you do today to meet the needs of what you need to do to make yourself happy?

_____

_____

_____

_____

_____

8. Discuss your WHY with someone you can count on with a new way of thinking about life, making different moves, and being accountable for your happiness!

_____

_____

_____

_____

_____

Your life depends on what you do to make it work in your favor. God has a plan all he wants you to do is to get still and Listen. Allow him to work through all the pain and hurt because he hears your cries. You are an overcomer do the very best you can at the moment. You always look to improve yourself in all that comes your way.

ABOUT THE AUTHOR

Who is Barbara J. Love now?
Who am I?
Barbara Love—a woman who exemplifies strength and integrity. Each day, I am striving to be a better person. I am a spiritual woman who believes in the power of prayer. I truly believe that, if it wasn't for God, I would not be writing this passage today. I'm a proud mother of four and a proud grandmother of three.
I am a Domestic Violence Advocate, Master Hairstylist, Salon owner of B Love B Beautiful Hair Salon, Entrepreneur, SCS Employee, Majorette Advocate to the Community, Veteran Foster Parent, Outreach Coordinator for my Church—The Common, Degree holder, CEO of The Love Foundation, Inc...and Loving Friend!

Made in the USA
Coppell, TX
10 August 2020